Options Trading

Beginners guide to get you started with Options trading

TABLE OF CONTENTS

INTRODUCTION 6
WHY OPTIONS TRADING? 7
CHAPTER ONE 8
    WHAT IS OPTION TRADING? 8
    TYPES OF OPTIONS 11
    THE BENEFITS OF TRADING WITH OPTIONS 14
    THE LEVERAGE INHERENT IN OPTIONS 15
    PLAYING THE DOWNSIDE WITH OPTIONS 17
    MANAGING RISK AND THE VARIOUS OPTION STRATEGIES 18
    PROFITING WITH OPTIONS IN OTHER SITUATIONS 19
    USING OPTIONS FOR INSURANCE 20
    OPTIONS STANDARDIZATION 21
CHAPTER TWO 23
    USING CALL OPTIONS FOR SPECULATIONS AND INCOME 23
    THREE EXAMPLES OF CALL OPTIONS 26
    THE LONG CALL STRATEGY – USING CALLS FOR 30
    SPECULATION 30
    THE BULL CALL SPREAD – AN ALTERNATIVE TO THE LONG 33
    CALL STRATEGY 33
    THE COVERED CALL – GENERATING ADDITIONAL INCOME FROM YOUR STOCK PORTFOLIO 35
    LONG-TERM SPECULATION – THE SPECIAL CASE OF LEAPS 40
    THE BEAR CALL SPREAD – COLLECTING INCOME FROM OPTION SELLING 41
    A WORD ON RISK MANAGEMENT 42
CHAPTER THREE 43
    USING PUTS FOR SPECULATION, INCOME, AND PROTECTION 43

THE LONG PUT STRATEGY – BETTING ON THE DOWNSIDE.. 44
THE BEAR PUT SPREAD – SPECULATING TO THE DOWNSIDE WITH SPREADS 47
GENERATING INCOME – SELLING NAKED PUTS 48
THE BULL PUT SPREAD – COLLECTING INCOME IN A BULLISH ENVIRONMENT .. 50
USING LONG PUTS TO PROTECT YOUR STOCKHOLDINGS 53
CHAPTER FOUR 57
   ADVANCED CONCEPTS AND STRATEGIES 57
   PRICING OPTIONS – WHAT'S A "FAIR" PRICE FOR AN OPTION? 59
   UNDERSTANDING VOLATILITY – OF VITAL IMPORTANCE TO OPTION TRADERS 60
   UNDERSTANDING THE GREEKS – MEASURING YOUR RISK 62
   RATIO SPREADS – BUYING AND SELLING UNEQUAL AMOUNTS OF OPTIONS 65
   INDEX OPTIONS – A USEFUL TOOL FOR INDIVIDUAL INVESTORS 68
   USING INDEX OPTIONS TO INSURE YOUR PORTFOLIO 71
   USING INDEX OPTIONS FOR SPECULATION AND DIVERSIFICATION 73
CONCLUSION: NOW YOU CAN ANSWER THE QUESTIONS "WHY OPTIONS?" 76

Copyright 2018 by George Graham - All rights reserved.

This document is geared towards providing exact and reliable information in regards to the topic and issue covered. The publication is sold with the idea that the publisher is not required to render accounting, officially permitted, or otherwise, qualified services. If advice is necessary, legal or professional, a practiced individual in the profession should be ordered.

- From a Declaration of Principles which was accepted and approved equally by a Committee of the American Bar Association and a Committee of Publishers and Associations.

In no way is it legal to reproduce, duplicate, or transmit any part of this document in either electronic means or in printed format. Recording of this publication is strictly prohibited and any storage of this document is not allowed unless with written permission from the publisher. All rights reserved.

The information provided herein is stated to be truthful and consistent, in that any liability, in terms of inattention or otherwise, by any usage or abuse of any policies, processes, or directions contained within is the solitary and utter responsibility of the recipient reader. Under no circumstances will any legal responsibility or blame be held against the publisher for any reparation, damages, or monetary loss due to the information herein, either directly or indirectly.

Respective authors own all copyrights not held by the publisher.

The information herein is offered for informational purposes solely, and is universal as so. The presentation of the information is without contract or any type of guarantee assurance.

The trademarks that are used are without any consent, and the publication of the trademark is without permission or backing by the trademark owner. All trademarks and brands within this book are for clarifying purposes only and are the owned by the owners themselves, not affiliated with this document.

INTRODUCTION

Options have become remarkably popular, especially in the U.S. Far from being confined solely to the institutions and professional money managers, options trading is now mainstream for "retail" traders from all walks of life. The concept of options is still, however, treated with fear and trepidation in some quarters. When I first embarked upon serious trading, a friend warned me about what I was getting into, but trading can be as safe as you want it to be. The simple fact is you need to have a trading plan that works. It needs to keep your risk low and your potential for reward high. You need your plan to have structure and simplicity so you can follow it every time. Over the years, my trading plan has become progressively simpler. To make it as a trader, it helps to develop the following traits in this book — and they can all be developed.

WHY OPTIONS TRADING?

The main reason for trading options is that for a smaller amount of money you can control a large amount of stock, particularly with call options. Call options are always cheaper than the underlying asset and put options usually are. Options are generally more volatile than their underlying instruments; therefore, investors get "more bang for their buck" or more action. Clearly this can lead to danger, but as you'll see, it also can lead to more safety and security. You'll also see that it can mean much greater flexibility in your trading and even give you the ability to make profit when you don't know the direction in which the stock will move.

Those investors with portfolios can set up protective measures in the event of a market downturn. It is also quite possible to set up a position whereby you can only make profit. Perhaps not a hugely exciting profit in triple digits, but a certain profit nevertheless. Options make this type of scenario possible.

In short, options give the investor added flexibility, potentially much greater gains for a given movement in the stock price, and protection against risk. On the flip side, used in the wrong way, options can lead people to serious losses.

You will be learning safe strategies only and the simple rules governing those types of trade.

CHAPTER ONE

WHAT IS OPTION TRADING?

An option is an arrangement where one grants another the right to buy or sell something in the future. In the case of Dow index future options, when one buys a Dow call options this entails that they are buying the right/privilege to purchase that underlying Dow future at a definite price at a specific time in the future. This definite price is called "strike price" while the specific time is called the "expiration date".

This trading can also be understood as when one investor buys a put, they are basically selling the market since a call fundamentally buys the market. In the same manner, when an investor sells a put, they are essentially buying the market since selling a call basically sells the market.

In order to have that chance to buy an option on this future, investors pay a so-called "premium." In case the market does not make the strike price of the option, then that option will be considered worthless on the expiration date. Moreover, in case the market does not reach the strike price of the option on the expiration date, it follows that the investor will be allocated the underlying future at that specific strike price.

How Options Trading Began

This market enterprise started in the 19 century. The beginnings of options trading coincided with the time when stock trading commenced. However, the scenario is different as newspaper advertising must be used at that time so that options buyers can find options sellers. It can be assumed that during that time options trading had not yet gained ground in the market.

Options trading started officially in 1848 when the Chicago Board of Trade was founded and options contracts began to trade in the United States. Other exchanges began to trade options when the Chicago Board of Trade, Kansas City Board of Trade, Minneapolis Grain Exchange and the New York Cotton Exchange commenced to trade contracts involving options.

Be that the case, options trading was still not popular as an option to invest into the market. The apparent reason for this low popularity is the low options liquidity during that time.

Significant changes came only in the middle of the 20th century when the Chicago Board of Options Exchange was opened and paved the way for options trading. Since then liq uidity of options grew tremendously making it as a pull factor for spectators to trade options.

Another important milestone was achieved in 1977 when options puts started to trade on the Chicago Board of Trade. In 1985 the NYSE and the NASDAQ began to trade eq uity options contracts.

Since then, options trading has been one popular way of investing into the market. The reason for this popularity is high liquidity and great leverage. Today, there is a wide range of the options that exist on the market. Options on equities, futures, indexes and currencies may be the considered by investors. Be that as it may, options trading is still regarded as one of the extremely high risky kinds of investment on the market where one may lose all invested capital.

Things You Need To Know About Options Trading

As mentioned earlier, options trading is highly risky if one is not equipped with great skills and basic knowledge about it. It pays a lot to know everything there is about trading options before you begin. If you are not equipped with enough knowledge and skill, you can lose a king's ransom in the first hours or days of the deal.

What you need to get is the proper and correct information in order to gain success in this venture. If you are given the wrong information, you can lose everything. So what should you do before you start trading options? First, be abreast with what options trading is all about. Give time to understand as much terminology used in this venture.

Knowing these terms will pay off later. In addition, knowing the difference between the types of options means a lot. There are two types of options. These two types are totally different. Don't ever confuse them as this might lead to you losing everything.

TYPES OF OPTIONS

The world of option trading may seem q uite daunting to a beginning trader, but in reality, there are only two types of options, Calls and Puts. Once you understand these terms, knowing which option to buy will become almost second nature. We will discuss these two types of options at a beginner level. It will not be very complicated nor will there be any horrible maths involved!

Calls

Call options can be thought of the buyer taking a bet that the underlying asset (i.e a certain parcel of shares, futures contract, etc) is going to rise in value. It gives the buyer the right, but not the obligation, to buy a certain asset for a certain price (called the Strike Price) before a certain expiry date. In essence, what you are doing is buying an opportunity. If you don't buy the asset before the option expires, you lose only the amount of money that you spent on the option, which is usually only a small fraction of the value of what the option controlled! You can always sell the option before it expires, either at a profit or to minimise a loss. Another choice is to exercise the option, which means you actually want to buy the asset it controls. As long as you have purchased the option, you can exercise the option at any point if it is an American-style option (European-style options can only be exercised on the expiry day)

Puts

Put options can be thought of as the buyer betting that that the underlying asset will fall in value. This type of option is an excellent instrument to have when you are trying to guard against losses in stock, futures contracts, or commodities that you presently own.

Put options give the buyer the right, but not the obligation to sell a specific q uantity of the underlying asset at a predetermined price (i.e. the strike price) during a certain period of time. Like call options, if you choose not to exercise a put option before its expiry date, the total amount of money lost is the price paid for the option.

However, as the price of the underlying asset drops in value, this drop in value is offset by the put option, which increases in value at the same rate the underlying asset is decreasing in value.

An easy way to look at put options is to think of it as an insurance policy. If you have an insurance policy on your home that costs

$500 for a year's protection from damage, if you go through the entire year without any damage, you have only lost $500. However, if your house is severely damaged (is has lost value), you can repair it (it maintain its value) with the insurance policy, which had only cost you $500, but paid for thousands of dollars in damage. The same thing can be applied to a share portfolio.

So that's all there is to it. If you think a share price is going to go up in value, buy a call option, as they increase in value with a rising market. If you think a share price is going to fall, buy a put option, as put options increase in value when the underlying asset price decreases.

THE BENEFITS OF TRADING WITH OPTIONS

A key benefit options offer over other investment vehicles is that an option trader can profit in either an up or a down market. When you buy an option, you are hoping that the underlying stock will move in the direction you want. If you're right, you make a profit. If you're wrong, you lose money. But it's really all a matter of two things: Time—since the option contract always expires at some point, and timing. Consistent with all forms of investing, timing is everything in options trading.

This book attempts to show how adding options to your trading arsenal can help you better reach your investment goals. How you use options depends on what you hope to achieve and how much risk you can afford to take. Some investors think of options only as a stand-alone and speculative product. And they can certainly be used that way. However, the potential uses of options go far beyond pure speculation—as we will endeavor to demonstrate throughout the book.

This work will cover a number of option strategies that illustrate how versatile options are in helping you meet your personal investment goals while also controlling your risk. If you want to protect long stock positions, discount your basis, leverage capital, or insure paper profits—an option strategy exists to help you. If you want to avoid as much risk as possible, some very conservative strategies are presented that will enable you to manage risk while also enhancing portfolio profits. Just as an experienced chess player sees the entire board and does not base strategies on the movement of a single piece, a well-informed investor is able to integrate options into a larger portfolio strategy

THE LEVERAGE INHERENT IN OPTIONS

Each option contract gives you the right to buy (a call option) or sell (a put option) 100 shares of stock at a specific price (the strike price) by a specific date in time (the expiration date). When you buy an option, you hope that the stock will move in your predicted direction, and quickly enough to make a profit. The cost of the option — the option premium — is far less than the cost of buying 100 shares of stock. For example, it would cost $6,000 to buy 100 shares of a stock currently worth $60 a share. If the option premium for a call option on this stock is $4, you could buy the option for only $400. That gives you the right to buy 100 shares of the stock — but you don't have to. That $400 gives you control over $6,000 worth of stock. That's leverage.

You get a different type of leverage when you buy a put. A put option gives you the right to sell 100 shares of stock, but you don't have to own the stock. The put buyer hopes the price of the stock goes down. If it does, the put becomes more valuable and can be sold for a profit.

As a pure speculation, buying calls or puts gives you the chance to make money on the movement of stocks, but without having to pay out big money at great risk. When you own shares of stock, the big risk is that the value might fall. So if you invest $6,000 in 100 shares of stock and its market value falls to $30, you then lose

$3,000. But if you buy a call option for a premium of $4, the most you will ever lose is $400. So while you control the same 100 shares of stock, you have only a fraction of the capital at risk.

Of course, using options in this way also entails risk. If the stock price does not move in the direction you anticipated, the value of the option will drop. Even if the stock price doesn't move at all, time works against you. The everlooming expiration date means that value goes out of the option day-by-day, and you can lose the entire premium paid for the option. So even while leverage is desirable, it comes with some amount of risk.

PLAYING THE DOWNSIDE WITH OPTIONS

Many stock investors think only with a bullish perspective. But as experience has shown, stock prices across the board can decline for long periods. Owning stock when this happens can be an expensive experience.

However, going long the stock is not the only way to invest in the stock market. If you think a stock will go down, you can sell the stock short.

Short selling stock is a potentially high-risk venture. When you short a stock, you believe the value will fall, and if you are right, you can then close out the short position at a profit. Short sellers open the position by borrowing the stock from their broker at a reasonable interest rate and then selling it on the open market. To close the position, they buy the stock back—the opposite of the traditional buy-then-sell pattern every stockholder knows. For short sellers, the risk is that their timing is wrong, and the market value of the stock rises. When that happens—it can cause big losses, which are theoretically unlimited. That's a very big risk to take—and short selling may not be an appropriate strategy for most stock investoors

However, put options in place of stock to play the down market presents the same opportunity, but with less risk. When you buy puts, you make a profit if the price of the underlying stock falls. So in a bear market, put buying can be profitable—assuming the timing is right. At the same time, your risk is limited to only the premium paid.

MANAGING RISK AND THE VARIOUS OPTION STRATEGIES

With options, you control how much risk you have. You can buy one option or several. You're not necessarily at the mercy of a fickle market that can make or break a portfolio with devastating results. You can manage your risk by putting in only as much as you want to expose to possible loss.

The main advantage stockholders have is that they can afford to wait out the market. Even if a stock loses half its value, the stock investor can just continue collecting dividends and wait for the market to go in the opposite direction.

While the option buyer may have less risk, they have less time also.

While some options like LEAPS may have a year or two until expiration, most options last only a few months. If you don't make your profit before expiration, you just lose. That's why it is so critical to have some basic options education—to familiarize yourself with all the various strategies available.

One of the great things about options is their versatility. There is a wide range of strategies available, and each of these strategies has a different risk/reward profile. Some strategies are high-risk, like the speculative buying of call and put options; others are designed to profit if specific future expectations are met. People who are unfamiliar with options typically view them as high risk, speculative investments, and overlook more conservative benefits many options strategies offer for:

(1) Protecting portfolio positions

(2) Spreading and hedging risk

(3) Generating additional income on your stock holdings.

These three strategies make options one of the more interesting and practical ways to invest, and they are especially useful when dealing with the challenges of volatile market conditions.

PROFITING WITH OPTIONS IN OTHER SITUATIONS

One of the significant advantages of options is their flexibility. When you own stock, you make a profit only if one thing happens: the stock's price moves above its current trading range. But options are so flexible that you can even make a profit if a stock stays within a limited trading range. Calendar spreads and short straddles are some of the strategies designed to produce profits if the stock price doesn't move. This means an option position can be profitable even if the stock shows very little movement in the period of time you have the position open.

Other strategies are designed to create profits if the stock price moves in either direction, such as long straddles. In this case, you don't really care what direction the stock price moves, as long as it does move. Because options can be used in so many combinations, their applications are very deep and rich. Once you understand how to use time as the key element in creating option profits, you will be well on your way to developing winning strategies that work specifically for you.

USING OPTIONS FOR INSURANCE

Options can also be used to "insure" your position. For example, if you buy one put option for every 100 shares of stock you own, it gives you downside protection. As the stock price drops, the put goes up in value. And no matter how far the stock price drops, you have the right to sell your stock at the strike price specified by the put option. You can also insure a short stock position. If you have sold stock short, the worst outcome would be a rising stock price. You can insure against that by buying one call option for every 100 shares you have sold short. As the stock price rises, the call goes up in value. And again, no matter how much the stock price rises, you have the right to buy the stock at the strike price specified by the call option. You can use options to insure your portfolio as a whole. There are options available on many different stock indexes, including of the drop in value of your stocks. the Dow Jones Industrial Average, the S&P 500, and the NASDAQ 100. Buying puts on the index that is closest to the composition of your portfolio gives you protection from market risk. When the overall market drops, it is likely that most of the stocks in your portfolio will also drop in price. But the index puts will gain in value, offsetting much, if not all,

OPTIONS STANDARDIZATION

Almost precisely. First, let me clarify that options do exist in the realestate market and they do work exactly as described above. The difference with options on stock is that you don't have to reach a detailed agreement with an individual seller in order to buy an option. Stock-market options are standardized.

This wasn't always the case. There was a time before "exchange-traded" options, and it wasn't that long ago. Options, in their current form, have only been around since 1973, and they've only gained their current level of popularity recently. For example, in 1999, the volume of options contracted traded in the U.S. stood at around 500 million a year. By 2006, that number had leaped to more than two billion.

Standardization is the key to making options widely accessible to individual investors. Whereas a real-estate option deals with a particular house, of which there is only one in the world, a stockoption contract deals with 100 shares of a given stock, for which there are millions exactly alike.

To understand what is meant by standardization, let's take a look at an example option quote:

Ticker	Strike	Esp.	Last	Bid	Ask
QXBHX.X	22.50	Aug	2.58	2.50	2.54
QXBHE.X	25.00	Aug	0.75	0.7	0.78

Above are two quotes for August options on eBay (Ticker: EBAY). At the time this quote was retrieved (July 28, 2008), eBay was trading at $24.78 per share. Each series of options has its own ticker symbol. A series is defined by three criteria: Issuer (in this case, eBay); strike price ($22.50 for QXBHX.X and $25.00 for QXBHE.X); and expiration (August for both series). The bid price of an option is the price at which you can sell the option; the ask price is the price at which you can buy the option. We're dealing with buying call options to start, so let's focus on the ask prices. Options are purchased in contracts, which, thanks to standardization, are always in terms of 100 shares. Therefore, one contract of QXBHX.X, with a $2.54 ask price, would cost you $254 (plus brokerage commission, which we will ignore until later in this guide). As the holder of that contract, you would have the right—but not the obligation—to buy 100 shares of eBay at the strike price, in this case $22.50, any time between now and expiration, in this case the Saturday following the third Friday of August.

Note: Options always expire on the Saturday following the third Friday of the month.

CHAPTER TWO

USING CALL OPTIONS FOR SPECULATIONS AND INCOME

Understanding the terminology and rules for options is necessary before you start trading them. Beyond that, you need to develop a thorough understanding of risk and how it varies from one strategy to another.

Remember that options can be used in a wide variety of strategies, from conservative to very high-risk. Many traders are first attracted to options for high-leverage directional trading.

Directional trading is when a trader believes he knows which way a stock price will move and opens an option position to take advantage of it.

With stock you only have to worry about one thing — price. In the landscape of options you have three shifting parameters: the price of the underlying stock, daily time decay, and volatility. Changes in any one of these will affect the value of your options. We have already mentioned how the value of calls and puts are affected by changes in the underlying stock price. Time is another concept that is fairly easy to understand.

The fact that options will expire and may become worthless in the future is an important and key feature in every option strategy; ultimately, it can determine whether your option trading decisions are profitable or not.

The effect volatility has on an options value is usually harder for beginners to understand. Ideally, what traders would like to know is what future volatility will be. But since we don't know that, we try to guess what it will be. The beginning point for this guess is statistical (sometimes called historical) volatility, or SV. The SV tells us what the actual volatility has been for this stock over a given period of time. However there is another measure of volatility called implied volatility, or IV, which traders use to decide if options are cheap or expensive.

There are different models for pricing options, but most will yield a price relatively close to each other. When you put in all the variables (stock price, time, interest rates, dividends, and volatility), you get an answer that tells you, based on those numbers, what an option should be worth.

But what if you work the model backwards? After all, you know what the option is trading at. You can also find out the other variables (stock price, interest rates, dividends, and time left in the option) with a bit of research. In fact, the only thing you don't know for sure is what future volatility will be.

When you put all those numbers in and work the pricing model backwards you get implied volatility, so named because it is the volatility implied by the actual option price. So IV is calculated based on the currently traded option premiums. Option traders often say that "Premium levels are high" or "Premium levels are low." What they really mean is that current IV is high or low. Once you understand this concept, then it makes sense that you should try to buy options when their premiums are cheap, and sell options when they are expensive.

Your approach to trading options should always be based on the level of risk you think is appropriate. Most investors use options as part of a larger strategy based on selection of stocks.

Thus, a study of fundamental and technical indicators is the logical starting point. Next we explain some basic option trading strategies using calls. We will explore the use of calls to speculate on the direction of a stock using both a simple call purchase and debit spreads. Then we will look at how you can use calls to generate additional income using covered call writes and credit spreads. We will talk a little about the special case of LEAPS, and how they can be used as a substitute for stock. Our goal here is to demonstrate how to increase your investing profits without exposing yourself to unacceptable risks.

THREE EXAMPLES OF CALL OPTIONS

If, for example, eBay went from $24.78 to $30, you — as the holder of one QXBHX.X contract— would have the right to purchase 100 shares at just $22.50 (the strike price). You could then turn around and sell them for $30 each, turning an investment of $254 into a quick profit of $496.

Here's how:

Your option contract, purchased for $254, gives you the right to buy 100 shares at $22.50. When the stock reaches $30, you exercise your option and buy 100 shares at $22.50 for $2,250. You then immediately turn around and sell them for $3,000. All said and done, you spent $2,504 ($254 + $2,250) and received $3,000, for a profit of $496 ($3,000 - $2,504).

Now what if the stock had instead fallen to $20 a share? Well, remember: Options give you the right, but not the obligation, to buy a stock at a given price. There would be no point in buying shares at $22.50 when you could buy them for $20 on the open market, so you would simply let your option expire worthless. You'd be out $254, but just as with shares of common stock, you can't possibly lose more than your initial investment when buying options.

Finally, let's look at what would happen if the stock stayed exactly where it was. eBay was at $24.78 when you purchased your option contract on July 28, and, in this example, after bouncing around for three weeks, it closed the third Friday of the month right back at $24.78. Well, your option contract gives you the right to purchase shares at $22.50, so you can still make $2.28 a share by exercising your option. You would thus make $228 ($2.28 * 100) and end up with a net loss of $26 ($228 - $254). Still, a loss of $26 is a lot better than a loss of $254, so it would make sense to exercise your option and mitigate your losses.

'In-the-Money' and Intrinsic Value

In the example above, you purchased an option that was in-the-money. In the case of a call option, that means the strike price is lower than the price of the underlying stock at the time it is purchased. An option that's "in-the-money" is said to have intrinsic value.

For example, an option with a strike price of $22.50 and a current stock price of $24.78 could be exercised immediately for $2.28 in per-share profit. It thus has $2.28 of intrinsic value.

But notice that the ask price for the contract is $2.54 per share. If $2.28 of the $2.54 is intrinsic value, what is the remaining $0.26?

Time Value

The difference between an option's ask price and its intrinsic value is commonly referred to as time value—although this is not a universally accepted term. Some traders prefer "speculative" value as an alternative, but for now, let's stick with the term "time value." How time plays a factor is obvious when one looks at options with the same strike prices but different expirations. For example, here are some more eBay option quotes:

Ticker	Striker	Esp.	Last	Bid	Ask
QXBHX.X	22.50	Aug	2.58	2.50	2.54
QXBIX.X	22.50	Sep	2.80	2.93	2.98
QXBIX.X	22.50	Oct	3.60	3.30	3.35
QXBAX.X	22.50	Jan	4.25	4.10	4.20

The only difference between QXBHX.X (with an August expiration) and QXBIX.X (with a September expiration) is their expiration dates, and yet the ask price for QXBIX.X (September expiration) is $0.44 higher. The ask prices for the later-expiring options are higher still. Why? Well, it should be obvious: The longer you have to exercise an option, the greater the chances that the stock will go up and thus give the option intrinsic value.

'Out-of-the-Money'

So far, the options we've been dealing with have been "in-the-money." Again, this means that the strike price of the call option—the price at which the holder of the option has the right to buy the underlying stock — is lower than the current price of the stock itself. Thus, the option has "intrinsic value."

But what about our other example from earlier, QXBHE.X? Let's review:

Ticker	Strike	Exp.	Last	Bid	Ask
QXBHE.X	25.00	Aug	0.75	0.7	0.78

If you bought a QXBHE.X contract, with a strike price of $25, you wouldn't want to immediately exercise the option. After all, you could buy shares for $24.78 — the current stock price, in this example — on the open market, so why would you want to pay $25 instead? This option has no intrinsic value, and thus the ask price of $0.78 is all time value.

So let's imagine you purchased one QXBHE.X contract for $78 ($0.78 ask price * 100 shares — remember, each options contract is for 100 shares) and the stock price of eBay hit $30 before expiration.

You could then exercise the option and buy 100 shares at $25 (the strike price) and immediately sell them for $30, thus making $5 profit per share. Your total net would be $422 ($5 per share * 100 shares - $78 for the option's premium) on an investment of $78 — a 540% gain.

One important concept: An out-of-the-money option is considered to have no intrinsic value — not negative intrinsic value. In the example above, with a stock price of $24.78 and strike price of $25, the option is considered to have $0 intrinsic value—not -$0.22.

THE LONG CALL STRATEGY—USING CALLS FOR SPECULATION

Most investors start by buying stock, and they are used to thinking in terms of purchasing a stock for its potential to go up in price. So new option traders usually start out simply buying call options because it seems similar to what they are used to doing. When a call option on stock is purchased (also called "going long the option"), the call holder is able to control the stock without actually possessing it, and does so for a fraction of the cost. Buying calls has been one of the most popular strategies with investors since listed options were first introduced. Before moving onto more complicated strategies, an investor should thoroughly understand buying and holding call options.

A long call is a leveraged alternative to the stock itself. As the stock price increases, the option value increases by more (sometimes much more) on a percentage basis. This leverage can result in large percentage profits, because purchasing calls requires a lower up-front capital commitment than an outright purchase of the stock. In fact your profits are theoretically unlimited, since there is no limit on how high a stock price can go. This strategy also has limited risk, since you cannot lose more than you paid for the option. However, while the potential loss is limited in terms of dollars, you can lose 100% of the premium paid for the call.

Calls with strike prices higher than the current stock price are called out-of the-money options; if the expiration date were today, they would be worthless. Out-of-the-money options have value only because there is still time left for the stock price to move above the strike price. The part of an option's price attributable to time is called time value or time premium.

At-the-money call option is one whose strike price is equal to (or in practice, very close to) the stock price. Again, the premium paid for an at-the-money option is entirely due to time. Of course, it won't take much of an increase in the stock price to turn this into an in-the-money option.

An in-the-money call option has a strike price that is lower than the current stock price. The difference between the strike price and current stock price, called its intrinsic value, is the amount the option is in the money. But as long as there is still time left until the expiration day, an in-the-money option will also have some time value as well. That means the price of an option can be broken down into two parts: intrinsic value and time value.

Stock price at $50

Call Strike ATM, OTM, or ITM	Option Price(s)	Time Value ($)	Instrinsic Value
60.00 Out-of-the-money	0.50	0.50	0.00
55.00 Out-of-the-money	2.00	2.00	0.00
50.00 At-the-money	4.00	4.00	0.00
45.00 In-the-money	7.00	2.00	5.00
40.00 In-the-money	10.00	0.50	10.00

The farther out of the money an option is, the cheaper it will be, and the higher the leverage. So if the stock makes a quick move in your favor, an out-of-the-money option will do the best job of multiplying your money. However, if this move does not happen quickly, the out-of-the-money option's performance is likely to disappoint you. At-the-money and in-the-money options move more like the underlying stock because their delta is greater. The delta of an at-the-money option is typically around .50 — meaning that a one-point move in the stock translates into a half point move for the option. In-the-money options have deltas approaching 1 and they move almost point-for-point with the stock.

Often the best balance of factors can be found using at-the-money, or just in-the-money, options.

There are several reasons to buy options. Those who would like to participate in movement of the stock price but lack the resources to buy it outright can buy an option for a fraction of the cost. The limited risk appeals to some investors that want to limit their downside to just the price of the option.

Finally, there are the people who trade options to take advantage of the leverage available when speculating on price movements.

THE BULL CALL SPREAD — AN ALTERNATIVE TO THE LONG
CALL STRATEGY

We mentioned that beginning option traders tend to start out buying calls. They should really consider the benefits of spreads. The bull call spread is used when you anticipate that the price of a particular stock will increase but want less risk than you get with a call purchase. It involves simultaneously buying a call option, while selling another call option at a higher strike price in the same expiration month. The biggest advantage of the bull call spread is that it lessens the effects of the two biggest enemies of long options—time and volatility. It is less sensitive to the day-to-day fluctuations in the stock price, so it is a more relaxed style of trading. The other benefit of a bull call spread versus the long call is that you risk less capital for an equal number of contracts.

That reduces your break-even point, and increases the probability of making a profit.

In a bull call spread, you buy calls at one strike price and sell others at a higher strike price. The calls you sell discount the purchase price of the calls you buy. For example, let's say a stock currently trading at $90 offers calls at the 100 and 110 strikes. The 100 calls cost $6 and the $110s are worth $4. So buying one of the 100 calls would cost you $600. But with the bull call spread, you could buy the 100 calls for $600 and sell the 110s for $400, which will cost you the net difference of $200. So for the price of a single call option, you could afford to buy three of the bull call spreads. So what is the full risk and profit potential of the bull call spread?

Worst case: If the stock price does not rise above $100 before expiration, you will be out $200 per spread for the whole transaction (plus trading costs).

Best case: If the stock price hits or exceeds $110 per share by expiration day, you will profit. Your gain will be the difference between the strikes ($10) minus the cost of the spread ($2) times the 100 shares, for a total profit of $800 for each spread you purchased.

THE COVERED CALL – GENERATING ADDITIONAL INCOME FROM YOUR STOCK PORTFOLIO

Covered writing is often touted as a safe way to generate extra income from a stock portfolio. It follows naturally from the simple purchase of stock, is relatively easy to explain, and results in immediate income.

And it seems to be just as safe as simply investing in stock. While speculative call buyers usually hold their position for a relatively short period of time, the covered call writer often expects to hold his position to expiration. The best part is that covered writers make money during periods when their stock holdings go nowhere. The income generated can be impressive, with annual returns of 30% or more. Remember though, such returns are possible only if the stock goes up or remains at around the same price.

There are two ways to sell calls, "naked" or "covered." A naked call exists when a sold call has no hedge or any position that mitigates or removes the risk. Owning 100 shares of the stock for every sold call option hedges the short position and removes some of the risk. The hedge could also be a long call at a different strike price, like in the bull call spread strategy discussed previously.

Remember also that an option is a contract, with different rights and obligations for buyers and sellers. When you buy a call option, it means you have the right to buy 100 shares at the strike price specified. When you sell calls, the owner of that call option can impose the right on you. If the option buyer chooses to exercise his rights, you as the seller have the obligation to deliver the specified number of shares at the specified (strike) price.

The danger of the naked call strategy is that the stock price might rise above the strike price of the call option you sold. In that case, you would be req uired to deliver 100 shares at the fixed strike price, which could be considerably lower than current market value of the stock. Therefore, the risk of writing uncovered calls is unacceptable for the majority of investors.

So you need to hedge a sold option in order to avoid that risk. When you own 100 shares of stock and you sell a call on that stock, the strategy is no longer high-risk. In the event of exercise, you own the 100 shares and can simply deliver them to satisfy the contractual demands of the exercised call. A covered call writer is primarily seeking income. They also receive some downside protection (by the amount of the premium received), but the tradeoff is that the maximum possible profit is limited by the sold call. But this can be a worthwhile strategy as long as you pick your strike price carefully. For example, let's say you originally bought 100 shares of stock at $36 per share.

You sell a 40 call and receive a premium of $2. Because you get $200 for selling the call, your basis in the stock is discounted down to $34 per share:

Original purchase price	$3,600
Less call premium	-200
Adjusted basis in stock	$3,400

In this situation, you will profit in the event of exercise, but your maximum profit is $6 a share (you receive $4,000 no matter how high the stock price at the time of exercise). If the stock price falls below $34, you would have a net loss.

Strike price x 100 shares	$4,000
Discounted basis in stock	-3,400
	$ 600

Once the call expires or is bought to close, you can then repeat the process by selling another call. This sequence can be repeated as often as you wish.

Covered call writers have a distinct advantage over writers of naked calls because exercise is not catastrophic. It simply means you keep the option premium, and sell your 100 shares of stock at a profit as well. You also continue to receive dividends as long as you own the stock. There are three possible outcomes to the covered call write:

1. You close the position. You can always cancel out a short position by a closing purchase transaction. In this case you begin with an opening sale; if the call option later declines in value, you can purchase it back and close the position. The difference between the "sale" and "buy" prices is profit, and reported as a short-term capital gain in the year the position is closed.

2. The option expires worthless. There is always the chance that a short out-of-the-money call position will never gain in-the-money value. As expiration nears, its time value begins to disappear q uickly.

At expiration, it becomes worthless. In that case, the entire premium is profit, and is reported as a short-term capital gain in the year the option expired.

3. The option is exercised. The third outcome is exercise. If the buyer were to exercise, your 100 shares would be called away at the strike price and you would keep the collected premium. This happens only if the stock price is higher than the strike price, thus making it an in-the-money option. Exercise can take place at any time, so if you sell a call you have to be prepared for this possibility. As a general rule of thumb, it makes sense to sell covered calls only if you are completely willing to have your 100 shares called away. However, if the stock's value rises and is close to the covered call's strike price, you might want to avoid exercise. You can do this by exchanging one call for another in an exchange called "rolling up." For example, you could close out the short call with a purchase transaction, and then sell another call option in a farther month with a higher strike price. You can roll up and out indefinitely as the stock price continues to rise as long as you are willing to continue using your 100 shares to cover the short call position.

Time is the friend of the option seller.

While time decay is a big problem for option buyers, it is the key to success for option sellers. The more the option value falls, the more you profit. The real beauty of selling covered options is not only that you can generate income with little additional risk, but the fact that you can repeat the process over and over. As each option position is closed or expires worthless, you can sell another call against the same 100 shares—and repeat that as many times as you like. So your 100 shares can produce profits not just from price appreciation and dividends, but also from call premium.

But there is some downside to the covered call strategy. First if the stock quickly goes up, even doubles or triples in price, your profit is limited. But of course you bought the stock in the first place expecting it to increase in value. And you were right! Unfortunately, in this case you will profit very little from it because your gains are limited by the call sold.

What if there is a significant drop in the stock price? Your calls really do very little to protect you against losses as the market falls. You get to keep the premium from selling the call (when it expires worthless), but you still own stock that is now worth much less than you paid for it.

Not everyone should sell calls, particularly those that expect very rapid stock price appreciation. Even though it is a profitable strategy, it works best as part of a broader investment program.

Understand exactly what possible outcomes could occur and be willing to closely monitor your positions so you can react if you need to. For those who do understand the covered call, it is a conservative strategy that can enhance investment returns significantly.

LONG-TERM SPECULATION – THE SPECIAL CASE OF LEAPS

LEAPS – Long Term Equity AnticiPation Securities – are options that have a far longer life than standard options, with a time frame of years rather than months. Only about 10% of optionable stocks have LEAPS, primarily the most popular high-volume stocks. LEAPS have significant time premium and are more expensive than standard options, but still cheaper than purchasing 100 shares of the stock. In many ways, you can think of them as a substitute for buying the stock.

LEAPS can also be used as a substitute for stock in strategies such as the covered call just discussed. In that strategy, you would buy the longer-term

LEAPS option and sell a shorter-term option on the same stock. The short option is covered, or hedged, with the long LEAPS option. Technically, this is really a horizontal, or calendar, spread. But many of the same techniques from the covered call strategy can be applied here, including the rolling of the short option as it is closed or expires worthless. And given the variations in time value, you can also profit from simply playing the timing of the spread. We will discuss the horizontal spread later in this book, and you should be familiar with the associated risks before trying it. The point, however, is that LEAPS provide great flexibility because of their higher time value.

THE BEAR CALL SPREAD — COLLECTING INCOME FROM OPTION SELLING

The bear call spread is a limited-risk strategy that essentially profits from the decay of time value. In one respect, it is the exact opposite of the bull call spread; you are hoping for a decline in the stock. You buy a bull call spread hoping its value will increase, not unlike a stock. But with the bear call spread, you receive a credit to your account when you place the trade, and your goal is to keep it. The credit received is your potential profit. You can never make more than that. You can lose it, however, and more if the stock moves up. You can even make money with a bear call spread if the stock price doesn't move at all between now and expiration. You just don't want it to move up.

To construct a bear call spread, you sell a call option at a lower strike price, and offset that by buying a call option at a higher strike price farther out-of-the-money. For example, let's say a $48 stock you think will fall in value has 50 and 55 call options available, with the 50 calls valued at $5, and the 55 calls valued at $3. Because the 50 calls will be closer to the current stock price, you will receive a net premium (or credit to your account) for this type of trade.

If the stock does fall in value, the 50 calls you sold will also decline in value. They can then be closed at a profit, or allowed to expire worthless.

The only reason to buy the calls at the higher strike price calls is to reduce your risk (and the possible loss) in case you are wrong and the stock goes up. That means your maximum risk exposure is equal to the difference between the strikes, minus the premium received when the bear call spread was opened.

The bear call spread in this example would be profitable as long as the stock finishes at or below $52 per share by the expiration date.

A WORD ON RISK MANAGEMENT

With all option strategies, you should know the potential loss as well as the potential gain before you enter a trade, and be willing to accept the loss if it does occur. Experienced traders who are successful year in and year out will attest that risk management is the key to long term profitability, particularly limiting the potential loss for each trade to a certain percentage level of your trading account. In interviews with some of these individuals, the figure most often cited is 5%, meaning that no trade should cost more than 5% of your trading account. A figure higher than this increases the odds that emotion will cloud your judgment. Your trading activity could then take on a character closer to gambling. Bottom Line: Manage risk wisely by limiting the potential loss from each trade to 5% of your trading account.

CHAPTER THREE

USING PUTS FOR SPECULATION, INCOME, AND PROTECTION

Americans are optimists; we think that everything is going to look better tomorrow, including stock prices. So we naturally tend to favor call options, because when the stock price goes up we will make a nice profit. In fact, when exchange traded options were introduced in 1973 there were no put options available, only calls! Put options on stocks didn't begin trading until four years later, in June 1977. The fact is, however, that the various stock markets (and the individual stocks they are comprised of) do not always go up, but can have long seasons of bearish activity.

In this chapter, we explain how to use two strategies — the long put and the bear put spread — when speculating on an expected drop in price. We will also look at opportunities to generate income by selling naked puts and credit (bull put) spreads when you expect a stock price to increase. Finally, we will examine how to use puts options to protect your stockholdings. The nature of puts makes them an ideal tool for hedging risk when you are concerned about downward price moves in volatile markets.

THE LONG PUT STRATEGY – BETTING ON THE DOWNSIDE

When you buy a put, you acquire the right to sell 100 shares of stock.

Like the call option, the put option is a contract that specifies the price (the strike price) you have the right to sell the stock at, and by what date (the expiration date). The put option buyer has the right to sell the stock at the strike price, but he doesn't have to. The put option seller, on the other hand, has the obligation to buy the stock at the strike price if the put is assigned. Most investors find it easier to understand calls, but the put gives the investor many advantages not available with calls. So the time spent learning about puts and how to use them properly is time well spent.

Many of the option terms used are the opposite depending on whether they are used with calls or puts. When talking about put options, in-themoney refers to a put whose strike price is higher than the current stock price. At-the money still describes an option whose strike price and stock price are the same, but an out-of-the-money put has a strike price that is lower than the current stock price. Just as in call options, the out-of-themoney put option position has higher leverage and more risk compared to an at-the-money or in-the-money option.

<u>Stock price at $50</u>

Put strike ATM, OTM, or ITM	Options Prices($)	Time Value($)	Intrinsic Value
60.00 In-the-money	10.50	0.50	10.00
55.00 In-the-money	7.00	2.00	5.00
50.00 At-the-money	4.00	4.00	0.00
45.00 Out-of-the-money	2.00	2.00	0.00
40.00 Out-of-the-money	0.50	0.50	0.00

As we saw earlier, an option buyer can only lose the amount paid for the option; nothing more. With the call option the profit potential was theoretically unlimited, since there is no limit on how high a stock price can go. But with a put option there is a limit, since the price of a stock can never go lower than zero. Still, that leaves lots of room to make a profit with most stocks. The same qualities of leverage, limited risk, and large potential profits that make buying calls attractive apply to put options as well. Just remember, the option buyer's enemy is time decay.

As each day goes by the option loses some of its value, so speculative put buying works best when you are working in a shorter time frame.

As with call options, there are many different strike prices and expiration dates available for put options. Since options with different strikes and durations respond differently to price movements in the stock, the decision about which option to buy is also important with puts. In no way should a cheaper price influence your decision about which option to purchase.

Remember, the cheaper option would be out-of-the-money (below the stock price), and buying them has a lower probability of success than buying at- or in-the-money options.

Also, remember that the time remaining before the expiration date is a key factor in the decision criteria. Time is working against the option buyer as soon as the order is executed. Decide how long you think it will take for the stock to make the expected price move. Now double it. That should give you a reasonable idea of what expiration month to consider.

Finally, always know the current volatility situation by looking at a volatility chart. This allows you to know whether the options are historically cheap or expensive for that stock. If implied volatility is very high, you may want to consider buying deeper-in-the-money options. These options have less time premium, so they are not as sensitive to changes in volatility. You may also want to consider using a spread to reduce your volatility risk in that situation.

The bear put spread, which is the subject of the next section, is a good alternative to straight put buying when speculating on a drop in price.

While the potential rewards from buying puts as a stand-alone strategy are high, never forget that the associated risk is very high as well.

THE BEAR PUT SPREAD—SPECULATING TO THE DOWNSIDE WITH SPREADS

Another way to play a down market is to use a bear put spread. The relative risks of an option purchase versus a vertical debit spread holds just as true with puts as when using calls. Those with bearish price expectations can buy a vertical debit spread with puts, called a bear put spread.

The bear put spread fixes the maximum loss and possible profit. As long as the possible profit is greater than the possible loss, you would consider the risk to be worthwhile.

A bear put spread involves buying a put option, and then selling a put option located farther out-of-the-money

The bear put spread has the advantage of fixing the maximum loss, but has the offsetting disadvantage of fixing the maximum profit. The same characteristics of higher commissions and slower development of profit relative to an option purchase applies to the bear put spread. With this in mind, it may not appeal to everyone, but beginning option investors are usually more comfortable with the risk profile of this trade and in return accept the limitations.

GENERATING INCOME – SELLING NAKED PUTS

One way to generate income with puts is to simply sell them outright. While earlier we said that selling naked calls was a high risk strategy that is inappropriate for most investors, selling naked puts does not carry the same type of risk. With the short put strategy, at-the-money or just outof-the-money puts are typically sold on stocks the investor wouldn't mind owning. If the stock stays around the current price, or advances, the investor keeps the premium when the option expires worthless. This strategy requires margin, so you have to put up enough cash in your brokerage account to "cover" the position in the event of exercise; thus, this strategy is also called the cash-secured put. What if the stock declines in price? In that case, the investor eventually gets assigned the shares, and the cost basis for his shares is the strike price of the put minus the premium received. That's why naked put writers should be prepared to buy the stock (and make sure they have enough funds available) before entering the position. For example, a stock is currently trading at $42.50. An out-of-themoney put with a strike price of 40 can be sold for $2.50, resulting in a credit to your account of $250. The $250 is yours to keep, no matter what. Worse case, you'll end up paying $4,000 for 100 shares of stock. Subtract the $250, and your effective basis is $3,750, or $37.50 per share. Not a bad deal! When you go naked with a put, you are hoping that the stock price will rise. It is a bullish position, and you have the same price expectations as you would when you buy calls. The difference, however, is that call buyers have to deal with time decay. They need the stock price to go up enough to cover the time value and produce a profit. Put sellers have time decay on their side, and are counting on time value to fall. A short put position can be profitable even if the stock does not move at all. So a key distinction between long calls and short puts is that it is more difficult to profit consistently from buying calls; it is relatively easy to profit consistently from selling puts. The reason: time value.

The decline in time value works against the buyer, but it is a valuable benefit to the seller.

Once you go naked on a put, you are exposed to the risk of having to buy 100 shares at the strike price. The owner of the put will only exercise it if it is in-the-money, which means you would buy the stock at a price above the current market value. That might not be a terrible outcome, as long as you consider the strike price a fair price for the stock. The market is full of inaccuracies, and there are often companies whose stock is under-valued. In those cases, having 100 shares put to you could still be a bargain, as long as you are willing to wait out the market.

When you sell a put, you receive a premium which is credited to your account. That is income, but it also discounts the price of the stock in the event of exercise. So if the strike price is $40, and you get a premium of $2.50 when you sell the put, your cost basis would be $37.50 per share.

Your opinion about a company's true value might influence your decision to take on the risk of the naked put. When you go naked on a call, your risk is potentially unlimited, because a stock can go up without limits; but when you sell a put, your risk is limited to the difference between the striking price and zero. In theory, as long as the company has assets greater than its liabilities, your "real" risk could be considered limited to the difference between the strike price and the company's tangible book value.

THE BULL PUT SPREAD – COLLECTING INCOME IN A BULLISH ENVIRONMENT

The bull put spread, like the bear call spread we examined earlier, is a useful tool for producing income. A bull put spread is a credit spread created by selling a put and then purchasing a put with the same expiration date at a lower strike price, farther out-of-the-money, on the same stock.

This strategy is best implemented in a moderately bullish market to provide high leverage over a limited range of stock prices. While the profit on this strategy can increase by as much as 1 point for each 1 point increase in the price of the underlying, the total investment is far less than that required to buy the stock. This strategy has both limited profit potential and limited downside risk, You would enter a bull put spread only if you feel confident the stock price will end at or above the strike price of the short put. You want to derive income from that opinion, and are willing to take a limited risk that you may be incorrect.

A big advantage of the credit spread over selling naked puts is the lower margin requirement. With the bull put spread, you only need to put up the difference in strike prices, less the credit received. For example, to create a bull put spread on a stock currently trading at $42.50, you could sell a 40 put for $7.00, and buy the 35 put for $5.00. You would need to maintain $500 in your account to cover the risk of this position.

But the net $2 premium is credited to your account, so it only costs you $300 to do the trade. By comparison, you would need to put up roughly $4,000 (or even more, depending on your broker's requirements) to sell a naked put at the 40 strike price. That's a big difference! To exit a bull call spread, you need to sell the higher strike put and buy back the lower strike put. Of course, if things go your way you can simply let the options expire. In that case, you keep the full premium received.

The maximum profit for the bull call spread occurs when the price of the underlying stock is above the strike price of the short put. If the stock price falls below that, and the option holder exercises the short put, you can exercise your long put to cover the assignment. In that case your loss is limited to the difference in strike prices, less the premium you received.

Debit and credit spreads formed using puts have performance curves that mirror those of call debit and credit spreads. The following list is a summary of the spreads we have seen so far:

Call debit spread Bullish

Call credit spread Bearish

Put debit spread Bearish

Put credit spread Bullish

There is little difference between the way debit spreads and credit spreads perform. Debit and credit spreads are directional trades with limited profit and limited loss. A credit spread can usually lose more than it can earn. Out-of-the-money credit spreads have the added advantage of being able to earn a profit as long as the market doesn't move too much in the opposite direction. The possible profit is equal to the credit received when you place the trade, while the maximum loss is equal the difference between the strikes minus the credit received. A logical exit strategy would be to close debit and credit spreads when they either lose or earn a fixed amount, set in advance, that you feel is acceptable.

USING LONG PUTS TO PROTECT YOUR STOCKHOLDINGS

If you hold stock in your portfolio, you naturally worry about the possibility that their value might fall. The potential volatility of the eq uity markets can be of great concern to investors. When discussing the covered call strategy, we mentioned that selling calls affords a small amount of downside protection (by the amount of the premium received). But buying a put to hedge the risk of owning stock, often called a protective put, gives the investor complete protection from a drop in the stock price below the strike price of the put. This strategy is actually more conservative than the simple purchase of stock. As long as a put is held against a stock position, there is limited risk. You know at what price the stock can be sold.

The only disadvantages are

- That money will not be made until the stock moves above the combined cost of the stock and the put.

- That the put has a finite life. But once the stock price rises above the total cost of the position, an investor has the potential for unlimited profit.

Buying a protective put involves the purchase of one put contract for every 100 shares of stock already owned or purchased. Purchasing a put against stock is similar to purchasing insurance in that the investor pays a premium (the cost of the put) to insure against a loss in the stock position.

No matter what happens to the price of the stock, the put owner has the right to sell it at the strike price of the put any time prior to expiration.

As with the covered call strategy, the protective put investor retains all benefits of continuing stock ownership (dividends, voting rights, etc.) during the life of the put contract, unless he sells his stock. If there is a sudden, significant decrease in the market price of the underlying stock, a put owner has the luxury of time to react. Remember that the enemy of any option buyer is time. The time value portion of the protective put will steadily decrease with the passage of time, and this decrease accelerates as the option contract approaches expiration.

But the investor employing the protective put is free to sell his stock and/or his long put at any time before it expires. For instance, if the investor loses concern over a possible decline in market value of his hedged underlying shares, the put option may be sold if it has market value remaining.

If the put option expires and has no value, no action needs to be taken; the investor will retain his stock. The only decision to be made is whether current market conditions still warrant protecting the stock. If so, simply buy another put farther out in time.

The put does not have to be purchased at the same time as the stock. A common way to employ the protective put strategy is to buy a put after the stock price has already increased. If an investor has concerns about downside market risk or is afraid the stock price might fall back in the short-term, he can protect his unrealized profits using a put, without having to sell the stock. The put can always be sold later for what value it has when the uncertainty has passed.

It should be clear by now that you can profit using options whether the market is rising or falling. Investors tend to favor calls over puts, but puts can play as important a role as calls in a well-designed investment plan. Both calls and puts can be used purely for speculation, to generate income, or hedge the risk of stock positions. Let's take the time to review the four basic approaches to using options, since every strategy or combination grows out of these:

- Using calls when you are optimistic. You believe the stock is going to rise, so you go long and buy call options. Other strategies include bull call spreads and covered calls when you own the stock.

- Using calls when you are pessimistic. You believe the stock is going to remain within a trading range or fall in value, so you go short and sell bear call spreads.

- Using puts when you are optimistic. If you believe the stock is going to rise, you can go short and sell naked puts; if the stock does rise, the put loses value and can be closed at a profit or allowed to expire. This should be done only if you believe the stock would be a good value at the strike price. Remember, if the stock price falls below that, the put could be exercised and you would have to buy 100 shares at the strike price. Alternatively, you can initiate a bull put spread.

- Using puts when you are pessimistic. If you believe a stock is going to fall in value, you can go long and buy puts or initiate a bear put spread. If you're right, the puts and/or spread will increase in value. If you own stock, you can also buy puts to protect against price drops on stocks in your portfolio.

In other words, there are a number of reasons to buy or sell options. Depending on the specific strategy, you can use them to speculate, produce income, or hedge risk. In some market conditions, buying or selling calls may not make as much sense as the corresponding use of puts. Thus, it is always wise to look at both sides—calls and puts—to find the strategies that will maximize your profits no matter what the overall market is doing. The beauty of options is that calls and puts in the right mix, or at the right time, can produce profits in any kind of market: up, down, or stagnant. There is always a strategy available that will produce profits.

CHAPTER FOUR

ADVANCED CONCEPTS AND STRATEGIES

Options can free you from the uncertainties of traditional investing practices. Now that you have a firm grounding in the basics of options trading, we will introduce some of the more advanced concepts and strategies. While we won't go into these with as much detail as we did call and put options, it is important that you appreciate the vast array of possibilities options make available to you, and that you begin to familiarize yourself with some of the concepts that all successful option traders need to master.

We will begin by spending a little time looking at three important concepts in more detail: option pricing, volatility, and the Greeks. The section on option pricing will give you an overview of the factors that go into determining what the "fair value" of an option is. The section on volatility explains its importance, and also introduces you to the historical volatility charts that allow you to see the current volatility situation for a stock. The next concept we will look at is how option traders measure the sensitivity of an option's price to changes in various factors, and we will define common terms like Delta, Gamma, Theta, and Vega; otherwise known as the "the Greeks."

Finally, we will briefly look at a number of advanced strategies, explain how they are constructed, illustrate their risk/reward potential with a graph, and discuss the price expectations and market conditions they will be the most effective for. There are three general market directions: up, down, and sideways. It is important to assess potential market movement when you are placing a trade. For example, if the market is going up, you can buy calls, sell puts, or buy the stock itself. Do you have any other choices? Yes. You can combine long and short options and the underlying stock in a wide variety of strategies.

These strategies are designed to limit your risk, while taking advantage of specific price expectations and market conditions.

PRICING OPTIONS—WHAT'S A "FAIR" PRICE FOR AN OPTION?

Fisher Black and Myron Scholes published an option pricing model, called the Black-Scholes formula, in 1973. This pricing model gave option traders the first practical way to quickly calculate what an option "should be" worth. While there have been improvements made over the years, some variation of this formula is still at the heart of most option pricing models today. We won't go into the mathematical details, but the main inputs into the model are Price (of the underlying stock), Time (left until the expiration date), Volatility (ideally, the stock's future volatility), the (risk-free) Interest Rate, and Dividends (paid over the time period of the option).

We have already looked at the impact the stock price and time have on the value of an option. How the price of the underlying stock affects an option's value is fairly straightforward. That the value of an option steadily decreases with the passage of time is also a relatively easy concept to understand, although you should be aware that option prices do not decrease in a linear fashion: the time premium erodes faster as the option nears the expiration date. Interest rates and dividends really have only a minor impact on the price of an option. But it is worth taking the time to look at the final input—Volatility—in a little more detail.

UNDERSTANDING VOLATILITY – OF VITAL IMPORTANCE TO OPTION TRADERS

It was mentioned earlier that volatility is often the most neglected of the major factors that influence option prices. We don't want to make that mistake here. Volatility is a vitally important consideration in options trading.

Every asset has q uiet periods when its options are cheap, and volatile periods when its options are expensive. Professional option traders are always aware of current volatility levels in relation to their historical context. To gain that perspective, they view historical volatility charts.

Volatility Charts are also useful for determining what "normal" volatility is. This can help you profit when current volatility temporarily goes much higher or lower than in the past. It can also be useful for spotting patterns in volatility you can take advantage of. The price of a stock can range from zero to infinity. Volatility cannot range that far. The investor can always count on volatility eventually returning to normal levels after going to an extreme. This principle is called "the mean reversion tendency of volatility." It may take anywhere from days to months, but sooner or later volatility always comes back to middle ground.

Generally, implied volatility tends to increase as stock prices decline, and decreases as the stock prices rise. The reason this occurs is because falling stock prices mean greater uncertainty with regards to future risk.

This leads to an institutional demand for insurance against future losses; meaning a higher demand for put options. This demand for puts drives implied volatility upward. On the other hand, increasing stock prices mean less uncertainty and subsequently less demand for put options resulting in lower implied volatility. This knowledge is very useful for option buyers. For instance, while the value of a call will increase with the stock price, the relationship between price and volatility means the call will lose some (sometimes a lot!) of its value due to the falling volatility.

It is good news for put buyers, however, because puts will increase in value from the double effect of falling prices and increasing volatility.

At times, implied volatility and statistical volatility will be in close agreement, while at other times one soars way above the other. You should always be aware of current news on the stocks you are trading.

Sometimes events can overwhelm historical volatility patterns. Be careful of situations where implied volatility is high and statistical volatility is extremely low.

These deals often freeze the target company's stock in a narrow trading range for a while. Meanwhile, the options may maintain high premiums because of the possibility of a sudden change in the deal. In general, unusual events can be treacherous for options traders — so be careful!

UNDERSTANDING THE GREEKS—MEASURING YOUR RISK

Because an option premium does not always appear to move in conjunction with the price of the underlying stock, it is important to understand the other factors that contribute to the movement of an option's price.

Options traders often refer to the Delta, Gamma, Vega, and Theta of their positions. Collectively, these terms are known as the "Greeks," and they provide a way to measure the sensitivity of an option's price to different factors.

These terms can be confusing and intimidating to new option traders, but broken down, they refer to simple concepts that can help you better understand the risk and potential reward of an option position. They cannot be looked up in your everyday option tables, but the best options software and online analysis sites automatically do the calculations and give you this information for every option and position you look at.

Delta measures the sensitivity of an option's theoretical value to a change in the price of the underlying stock. It is represented by a number between 0 and 1, indicating how much the value of an option will increase when the stock price increases one dollar. Delta is a very important number to consider when constructing spreads and combinational positions.

Call options have positive deltas and put options have negative deltas. At-the-money options generally have deltas of around .50. Deeper in-the-money options might have a delta of .80 or higher. Out-of-the-money options have deltas as small as .20 or less. Delta will change as the option becomes further in- or out-of-the money. When a stock option is deep in the money, it will begin to trade like the stock—moving dollar for dollar with the underlying stock, while the far out-of-the-money options don't move much.

Since Delta is such an important factor, the marketplace is interested in how Delta changes. Gamma measures the rate of change in the delta for each one-point increase in the underlying stock. It is a valuable tool in helping you forecast changes in the delta of an option or an overall position.

Gamma is largest for the at-the-money options and gets progressively lower for both in- and out-of-the-money options. Unlike Delta, Gamma is always positive for both calls and puts. Delta and Gamma change constantly. The factors that affect Delta and Gamma are the same ones that affect an option's value including time, the price of the stock, and volatility.

The next Greek we will look at is Vega, which measures the sensitivity of the option's price to changes in implied volatility.

Although implied volatility changes affect whole option chains, each option has its own Vega and will react by varying degrees. For instance, the impact of volatility changes is greater for at-the-money options than for the in- or out-of-the-money options. Longer-term options, especially LEAPS, have higher Vega, and thus their value is more sensitive to changes in volatility.

Finally, Theta is a measure of the time decay of an option. It is the dollar amount that an option will lose each day. For at-the-money options, Theta increases as an option approaches the expiration date. For in- and out-of-the-money options, theta decreases as an option approaches expiration.

Theta is one of the most important concepts for a beginning option trader to understand because it explains what effect time has on the value of purchased or sold options. The further out in time you go, the smaller the time decay.

The Greeks can help you quantify the various risks of every trade you are considering, but it is important to realize that these numbers are strictly theoretical, and that the values are based on mathematical models. The Greeks provide an important measurement of the risks and potential rewards of an option position. Combining an understanding of the Greeks, with the insight that risk graphs provide, lets you take your options trading to another level.

A wide variety of option strategies exist which combine calls, puts, and the stock itself. These strategies exist, cover every possible scenario, and market environment. Some are created from options of just one type (calls or puts), while others use both in combination.

RATIO SPREADS — BUYING AND SELLING UNEQUAL AMOUNTS OF OPTIONS

Up to this point, every spread strategy we have shown involved equal amounts of long and short options. But there are also ratio strategies, where the number of long options and short options are not identical.

One useful ratio strategy is called the backspread. It is perfect for times when you expect a big price move, but at the same time know that you could be wrong and no move will develop.

A backspread is constructed by shorting a near-the-money option, and then buying a larger number of the same type of options (calls or puts) at a strike price farther out-of-the-money. The most common ratio is one by two, and you should try to choose the options in such a way that the option you're shorting brings in a credit that covers the cost of the options you're buying, resulting in no net cash flow, or even a small credit to your account.

The call ratio backspread is a hedged directional trade where we expect to profit from a strong upward movement, while hedging our downside. If the stock price does rise, you will profit from the upward price movement — similar to a long call position. If your expectations turn out to be wrong, and the market moves against you, this is positioned in such a way that you either do not lose, or may even move into a small profit zone.

Since you are net long options, the profit potential is unlimited. And since the sale of the more expensive options pays for the options you purchase, it costs you nothing if both legs expire worthless. The short leg of the backspread also helps reduce time decay as a worry. However, there is a catch. There is a price zone where the backspread loses money, and it occurs if the stock moves in the desired direction by only a small amount. But it takes time for the maximum loss to develop, so that risk can be offset somewhat by using longer-term options. Then if the hoped-for big move fails to materialize in a reasonable amount of time, you can close the position for a small loss. Note that if you are bearish, backspreads can be constructed just as well with puts, and behave in a mirror image fashion to call backspreads.

In this final section we will explore index options, and how they can be used as part of your overall investment strategy. Then we proceed to give some suggestions on how to initially approach options trading.

Different forms of options are used everyday. You have insurance on your house and car to protect your property from an unlikely catastrophe, for which you pay a small amount known as the premium. In the same way, investors can buy index options as insurance for stock holdings.

Capital preservation can be every bit as important as capital appreciation to your long-term investment returns. Sure, every investor would prefer to have consistent gains all the time, but events outside your control can cause a temporary drop in the value in your investments. Stock options allow you to hedge the risk of individual positions, while index options let you protect the value of your portfolio as a whole from unforeseen events.

INDEX OPTIONS – A USEFUL TOOL FOR INDIVIDUAL INVESTORS

Prices of index options are based on a broad segment of the market, rather than on an individual stock. Stock options give you the right to buy or sell 100 shares of an individual stock. With index options, however, you cannot sell partial shares of hundreds of stocks, so "exercise" always means getting the difference in cash between current value and the strike price. But most of the same terms, strategies, and concepts we have already studied apply just as well to these instruments.

The concept of index options began in 1983, when the Chicago Board Options Exchange (CBOE) began offering options on an index of 100 stocks. This was called the Options Exchange Index, and is abbreviated OEX. Today, this index typically trades over 100,000 contracts worth over $20 million every day, and is still in the top ten of the most active options. Options are also available for the Dow Jones Industrial Index (DJX), the S&P 500 (SPX), the Philadelphia Semi-Conductor Index (SOX), the NASDAQ 100 (NDX), and dozens of others indexes tied to a particular market or sector.

Index options can be used to speculate on the future price movements of these markets, and most of the same strategies we went over with stock options can be applied. However, here we will focus on the use of index options to insure, or hedge, a portfolio against a broad market decline, while at the same time allowing that portfolio to participate in any market advance.

Institutions and mutual funds are the biggest customers for index options.

They manage large diversified stock portfolios, and it is easier for them to purchase puts on an index or sector rather than purchasing them on hundreds of individual stocks.

When analyzing how to hedge their risk, they must balance the cost of the strategy against their opinion of the market. Index puts are not cheap, so why are these managers willing to risk underperforming the market by 3% during a 90-day period (approximately a 13.2% annual rate)? The manager is willing to take that risk if he or she has a bearish view, and hopes to beat the market by profiting from the puts. The objective of the index option purchase is to limit or insure against portfolio losses.

Volatility is an important measurement of risk, and index options have lower volatility than options on individual stocks. When you trade an index option, your profit or loss is not due to the movement of a single stock. The overall mix of the index determines its value, and this has a smoothing effect on price changes. The "averaging" effect on index options means that they tend to typically trade in a more narrow range (percentage-wise) than the range for many component stock options.

Another feature that makes index options less volatile is that they are not as subject to company risk.

A single event, such as a merger, or an unexpectedly low earnings report, will not affect the index as much as it does the individual stock. Just as a mutual fund delivers a more consistent return using a large portfolio of stocks, the index also benefits from this same diversifying effect relative to its component stocks.

USING INDEX OPTIONS TO INSURE YOUR PORTFOLIO

The techniq ue of hedging your portfolio is straightforward. Find the index with the composition that most closely resembles your own portfolio, and then purchase out-of-the-money protective puts. But unlike stock options, where you know you need to purchase one put for every 100 shares of stock you own, your portfolio is unlikely to have precisely the same stocks as the index, and not in exactly the same proportion.

There are measures like portfolio delta that allow you to come close, but hedging an individual portfolio is still a bit of an art. The unusual part of this strategy is your objective: purchase puts, and then hope they expire worthless!

Strange as it may sound, a portfolio manager actually hopes that his outof-the-money put options expire worthless. After all, an honest homeowner does not hope that his house burns down so that the insurance policy will pay off. Similarly, a portfolio manager who buys out-of-themoney puts doesn't hope the market declines so that his portfolio will decrease in value by less than the overall market. This is a hard concept for many investors to understand. But an experienced money manager recognizes there are times when a sharp market correction, while not expected, has a high enough probability of occurring to justify the expenditure of 1% to 3% of the portfolio on out-of-the-money puts for 1 to 3 months of insurance.

You can also use index options to insure other positions, to a degree. For example, if you have invested part of your portfolio in shares of a mutual fund, you could buy index option puts to protect your shares in the event of a downturn in overall value.

The match might not be exact, but the strategy has a specific purpose: to anticipate and protect against broad declines of the type we have all seen in recent years. Markets do tend to move generally in the same direction, so that stocks—even those whose individual fundamentals are strong—decline when the overall market does. By the same argument, a strong bull market tends to pull most stocks in an upward direction, including under-performers, at least to some extent.

USING INDEX OPTIONS FOR SPECULATION AND DIVERSIFICATION

Index options can also be used for speculation. Here they offer the advantage of diversification, helping you to avoid the all too common mistake of simply picking the wrong stock. It is possible to time your decision well but pick the wrong equity. So while a sector might perform strongly as a group, the one exception could be the stock in which you invest all your capital! Diversification has been the major appeal of mutual funds for equity investors; and it works equally well for option investors or speculators. Some people think that owning shares of five different stocks is enough diversification; but in a weak market, all five might fall in value. Other investors believe that a sensible alternative is buying shares of mutual funds. However, mutual funds have a number of drawbacks:

1. Management charges a fee. Every mutual fund charges an annual fee, a percentage of the portfolio that goes to management salaries. This fee is charged whether share values rise or fall. With index options, you pay a transaction fee on both sides, but other than that, you keep all your profits.

2. A Load might apply as well. Many mutual funds are also subject to a load fee, as much as 8% of all the capital you invest. So for every $100 you put in, you have only $92 at work. The load fee discounts your investment, even when the fund performs poorly. Why pay a sales commission? If you're sophisticated enough to

consider options, you don't need to use a mutual fund salesman to tell you where to have historically performed on a par with the load funds, and you don't need to support a salesperson in addition to putting your capital at risk.

3. You're still putting capital at risk without leverage. When you buy shares of mutual funds you're buying at 100% levels, with no leverage. That means that all of your capital is at risk at full price. So if the value of the fund falls, you have lost money. In recent years, millions of investors have found themselves invested in funds whose current market value is far below their invested value. They either sell at a loss or sit tight and wait for the market to turn around — just to get back to their starting point. With index options, this problem is avoided because your only risk (in long positions, at least) is the amount of the premium paid, which is a fraction of the index values you control.

4. Equity diversification can work against you. One of the "dirty little secrets" on Wall Street is that diversification is not always a profitable tactical move. If the overall market performs poorly, even a well-diversified portfolio is likely to lose value. For an investor who does not understand how the market works, diversification (using mutual funds) provides some comfort.

However, only a small portion of all equity funds actually beat the overall market. The impressive long-term returns claimed in mutual fund brochures are generally the result of reinvested dividends and capital gains, not because the fund has some great insight into which stocks to buy.

As a general rule, investors tend to think only in terms of timing for upward price movement. Everyone wants to buy low and sell high. But whether you use individual stock options or index options, don't overlook the importance of the put. If the market trend is downward, you can make as much money, or more, buying puts than you can when you buy calls hoping for a reversal in price movement. Most investors are incurable optimists, and tend to think of puts only for insurance or as part of other strategies designed to profit when prices go up.

CONCLUSION: NOW YOU CAN ANSWER THE QUESTIONS "WHY OPTIONS?"

We started this book asking the question: Why options? We have tried to answer that question using specific examples, and hopefully you are beginning to feel comfortable with the idea of using options in your daily investment routine. Options open up a lot of possibilities; opportunities for leveraged speculation, conservative income generation, and also portfolio insurance.

So why is it that options often are considered riskier than stocks? The difference, of course, is time. Because options often expire worthless, you can easily lose all your investment. That is why it is important to understand both the risk and potential rewards of any option trade before you enter it, and today's technology actually allows every trader, private or professional, to evaluate a proposed option trade with amazing speed and relative ease.

Computer software that models the behavior of option trades can help tremendously. It is entirely possible to trade options without the help of computers and financial software. But why would you, when you'd be at such a disadvantage? Options analysis software does all the calculations for you, and displays risk graphs that let you quickly make essential trading decisions. There is a significant benefit to seeing all the potential outcomes graphically, including how a position will respond to movement in the stock price, to time decay, and to changes in implied volatility.

www.ingramcontent.com/pod-product-compliance
Lightning Source LLC
Chambersburg PA
CBHW070210230526
45471CB00002B/910